# How to Deal with Loneliness in A Relationship

A Short Note for Overcoming the Feelings of Isolation and Finding Fulfillment

**Claire Robin**

# Table of Contents

# Introduction

Experts do agree that loneliness is a human emotion that can be both unique and complex to different individuals. A young guy who struggles to make friends at his college in a foreign land has different needs than a lonely widower who lost his wife recently. To grasp the full meaning of loneliness, it's necessary to look at exactly what we mean by the term "lonely," as well as the different causes, health hazards, and how it can be treated.

Loneliness is a state of mind which causes people to feel unloved, empty, alone, and unwanted. Lonely people often yearn for human contact, but their state of mind makes it more difficult for them to connect with other people.

Many experts believe that loneliness is not necessarily about being alone, but instead, it is about the feeling of being empty, unwanted, isolated because it plays into one's state of mind. For example, a university first timer might feel lonely amid roommates and other peers. A clergyman beginning his evangelical ministry might feel lonely after being deployed to a foreign land, despite being constantly surrounded by other members of the clergy and the laity.

Factors contributing to loneliness include situational variables, such as physical isolation, relocating to a new environment, death of a loved one, or divorce. People who lack self-confidence often believe that they are unworthy of attention or regard of other people, and this can lead to isolation and unending loneliness.

Being alone sometimes can be healthy for us. The trouble is actually when we are in a relationship and still feel the same because we think we are not getting enough psychological support from our partners. To put forward a simple definition of loneliness; it can be defined as a damaging emotional condition, developed as a result of the real or supposed absence of good social interactions.

# CHAPTER ONE: What Loneliness Entails in A Relationship

Some people tend to believe that once you are engaged in a relationship, your feeling of loneliness will be a thing of the past. They believe it's no longer possible for you to feel lonely when you have your partner on your side to support you, care for you, and motivate you. Many people often feel isolated in serious relationships, as time and change in circumstances can put pressure on your union and lead you to feel far-away from your partner.

People become lonely in relationships for many different reasons, but most often, it has to do with the feeling of disconnection from their partners. Once a person becomes disconnected, the loneliness begins to creep into their lives, and cause them to feel hurt and uncared for.

1)    Lack of physical connection

It's natural to feel lonely in a relationship if you feel emotionally or physically ignored by your partner. If you don't think that your needs are being met and that perhaps your partner doesn't seem to care about you anymore. This can be, in a sense, likened to the feeling of being unloved and undervalued. This can cause loneliness and create an invisible barrier between partners.

2)      Inability to uncover what you want in a relationship

Sometimes, we can become lonely when we are looking for someone or something else in a relationship. If you don't know what you are looking for in a relationship, then it is unlikely for you to be happy and fulfilled. If it is not the kind of man you thought you are dating because you are the flashy type and your man is homely or you are the party type and your man is the workaholic type and you both don't agree on crucial issues, relationship issues will linger on. You must know exactly what it is you want in a relationship in order to fully embrace and engage with your partner.

3) Lack of open and honest communication

Loneliness can also occur when communication is not frank and sincere. You need to talk to your partner honestly, and let him/her know how you're feeling. Perhaps your partner doesn't realize you're feeling isolated, or unfulfilled. When you read the mind of your partner, you might not be right in your assessment, so asking caring questions may bring out all the useful responses that can easily strengthen the bond of the relationship.

Do you have the same interests, morals or hobbies? Can you agree on essential things that bind you both?  If not, it could be that you are not compatible as you previously believed, and it might be the root cause why you are longing for something different.

# CHAPTER TWO: Causes of Loneliness in A Relationship

Loneliness rears its ugly face when in a relationship, you both are in a secluded place, but cannot connect. You both feel awkward to be together alone. There is neither physical nor emotional intimacy between you. This is a typical example of what loneliness is all about. In simple words, you both are a couple to the whole world, but not for yourselves.

These are some of the causes of loneliness in a relationship.

I.      Maltreatment by one of the partner

Your spouse feels that he/she is all powerful, influential, and probably the breadwinner. He bullies you around and keeps you under constant check and fear. Psychological and emotional abuse becomes a regular feature of the relationship. He instills fear in you, and you are constantly afraid because you do not know what circumstance will stimulate his temper and invite wrath. This keeps you away from him as much as possible, and even when you are together, you hardly speak to him lest he not flare up and deal with you in the usual way.

II.    Work overload:

Reasons advanced for divorce cases nowadays are a busy schedule of both or one of the couples. You both are so busy with your careers or with other family matters that you hardly get the time to spend together. Pursuing your career is absolutely important but entirely at the expense of your marriage or other relationships. You must create quality time to be together and open a wide channel of communication when you are far away from each other. These channels can be texts, Whatsapp or other social media channels.

If these are not done, it creates a vacuum between the couple which widens over time

III.    Longing for emotional support:

You received a message that your father has been rushed to the hospital suffering from a cardiac attack, and as a result, you are highly worried. However, your spouse downplays the pains you are going through, and instead, he goes out drinking with friends at the usual joints. The emotional torture can be worst if your spouse is the breadwinner of the family.  When there is no emotional connection, there is hardly any scope for emotional support. So, when you know you will not get the support from your man, you would prefer maintaining silence to sharing your emotions—since sharing will cause you more agony.

IV.    Lack of physical intimacy:

Couples that are emotionally disconnected hardly get physically intimate with each other. The question is; when was the last time you gave your partner a passionate kiss, let alone making love to her. A kind word or a warm hug or a steamy night is not just for the body but for the mind too. Even a story of how you fared in the office that day is sufficient to begin to re-enkindle some life into the relationship. The lesser you do them or not doing any of them at all is an invitation to widen the gap between you and your partner.

V.    Lack of quiet time together:

You always attend to your kids and sometimes other family members. Or perhaps the family is so big that you both cannot make out time for a few moments with your partner. Initially, you try to make out time to be together with your spouse, but that fails, then you suspend making further attempts indefinitely. You cannot give up too early if you want to maintain the relationship. You have to try over and over again and if needs be, consult your partner to assist in creating the time for you both. Since you don't want to lose your marriage or relationship, you must steal the time even at the expense of other equally important engagements.

VI.    Knowledge from the past:

Loneliness after marriage does not always come from your spouse. Some past events or relationships in your past life can also contribute enormously. Research studies also confirm that your loneliness can be the result of depression or hostility with your parents or siblings and your past relationship with them. A girl who was violently raped at a tender age may live with the horrible memory all the days of her life and may affect the current relationship. So, you must examine your life thoroughly to discover how your present predicament emanated.

VII. Nagging partner

A partner that nags should examine him/her self before complaining about loneliness. Most people dislike nagging and would prefer to stay out of the home, either to delay coming from work or to leave the house at the slightest provocation in the form of nagging. Instead of asking your partner, " how was the day, did you have a hectic day in the office, instead, you will be asking, "what did you get for me from the supermarket, I would rather prefer takeaway food to home-prepared food." Don't think nagging is going to take you somewhere in your relationship. No matter how good your spouse is, nagging irritates and has the potential of wrecking his day and even the marriage eventually.

# CHAPTER THREE: Why You Need to Deal with Loneliness

Loneliness can threaten your physical and mental health, as the thoughts of marital separation or abandonment heightens the risk of potential health hazards. In our society today, it is frowned upon to keep aloof. The family sometimes encourages you to look for a partner and eventually get married. Some people still do things on their own, go to places by themselves such as movies, concerts, shopping malls, and even church service, even while surrounded by family, spouse, friends, and associates. It is perfectly acceptable to be lonely.

We shouldn't be afraid to be alone even though it exposes us to vulnerability and feeling of abandonment. It is true we need others because others make us complete, take care and love us. Perhaps you may think lonely people are weird. You may think that you do not have reasons to be lonely because you have a lot of love to dish out and you don't have anyone by your side.

However, loneliness can have negative effects on your life if you leave it unchecked. It can be taxing both psychologically and physically and can be accompanied by some devastating illnesses which will have a long-lasting effect on your body unless you make conscious efforts to disengage from the feeling. Some of the health problems associated with loneliness are listed below.

**Dangers of loneliness**

- Feeling of loneliness can trigger depression

- Chronic loneliness heightens the risks associated with cardiovascular disease and stroke.

- Tumor consequences are likely to worsen.

- There is likely to be a reduction in participation in social activities, exercises, and leisure.

- Loneliness can increase stress because of the lack of emotional support.

- Loneliness can trigger the blood pressure to rise (HBP)

- It can also cause impairment to memory and the process of learning.

- It may lead to poor decision making.

- It may directly affect cognitive impairment, and the risk of Alzheimer's disease is likely to develop or increase.

- The function of the brain may be altered as a direct consequence of loneliness.

**Apart from the areas mentioned above, loneliness can also affect your life in other ways:**

Lonely adults appear to take more alcohol and indulge in substance abuse and get less exercise compared with those that are not lonely. Lonely people appear to consume a diet that is higher in fat, don't normally have a sound sleep and yet have more day-time fatigue. It has also been reported that loneliness disrupts the regulation of cellular processes deep in the body, exposing us to premature aging.

There is evidence that correlates the low level of loneliness with marriage, higher economic status, and higher educational levels. Higher levels of loneliness are heightened by physical health symptoms, living a single life, small or no social network, and low scale social relationships.

## Benefits of dealing with loneliness in a relationship

Human beings are social species, and so we need others, but to be good with others, we must first be good with ourselves. Before we talk about the benefits of dealing with loneliness in a relationship, it may deem necessary to talk about the benefits of being lonely since it can be good for us to be lonely sometimes.

Spending time being alone is an opportunity for us to think. It makes us to get to know who we are, to connect with ourselves, and it is important for our personal development.

Some people find it difficult to spend time alone. The huge dependence on others to enable us to carry out our functions in life, in addition to being a sign of emotional complications, does not give us the chance to be cheerful. It can't be absolutely normal if you tend to rely on others to be happy, we must be answerable for our happiness.

Seclusion allows us to think about and know what we want to do with our lives, what we want to achieve in life, what we enjoy doing, what we don't like, and where to focus our attention.

Creative ideas come to us naturally when we are alone, so spending time alone and being in a brainstorming session can bring out all the creative prowess locking inside us. This is because when we are alone, we can let our minds roam freely and we are better able to pay attention to ourselves.

The benefits of dealing with loneliness in a relationship/

• Dealing with the feeling of loneliness can make depression go away

- The risks associated with cardiovascular disease and stroke may never arise if loneliness is dealt with as soon as it occurs.

- Tumor consequences may not rear its ugly face if loneliness is dealt with.

- With the problem of loneliness effectively dealt with, there is likely to be normal participation in social activities, exercises, and leisure.

- You are not likely to suffer stress because you enjoy emotional support.

- There is no reason for you to suffer high blood pressure unless for other underlying reasons.

- Your memory and processes are not likely to be adversely affected.

- Your decision-making ability will be enhanced.

- Your cognitive impairment and the risk of Alzheimer's disease are not likely to be affected.

- Your brain may function effectively and efficiently if you don't have the symptoms of loneliness.

- You are not likely to be a victim of alcohol or drugs abuse

# CHAPTER FOUR: Steps to Deal with Loneliness in A Relationship

The difference between being alone and lonely, and being in a relationship and lonely is very clear. Alone is intentional, where we might be at ease and fulfilled, but loneliness is a helpless situation. One of the reasons why we go into a relationship is to be sheltered from the feeling of loneliness. Relationships should make one have a sense of 'wholeness,' and if you don't feel that way, then it is obvious that things are not right in the relationship. Your bond does have some major issues to be resolved.

Many people in a relationship feel lonely at a particular time in their lives. Loneliness in a relationship does not happen all of a sudden; it develops gradually over time. Maybe your partner is under pressure from office work. Lately, he doesn't come back home early enough. Or simply, perhaps you both have run out of steam to talk about something (often in situations where you do things together). Gradually you begin to communicate in a transactional tone. For example, "John and his wife, Betty, are here this afternoon, "I will be off to the supermarket immediately after breakfast." Please don't forget to call the electrician to come and fix up the electric cooker".

When things begin to develop this way, you don't need a prophet to tell you that you are drifting away from your partner and it will not be long before you both will spend the evenings or weekends doing different things. He may go to the movies while she goes for outdoor games. Dealing with loneliness in a relationship requires taking positive initiatives by one or both parties to defuse the tension.

i.    Research the root cause of the loneliness

Try to understand the root cause of the loneliness. Loneliness in a relationship is caused by something else that is going on between the couple. The only true solution to loneliness is unraveling its root cause. Once you are able to do that, you can work towards uprooting the cause at the source, and loneliness is likely to be a thing of the past.

ii.    Be independent

One of the problems people create for themselves in a relationship is to be completely dependent on their partner's financial support and emotional fulfillment. It is vital that you give yourself sufficient attention just the same way as you expect the attention of your partner. There are certain things your partner will not be able to provide for you; it is an opportunity to provide them by yourself.

Some of us have possibly at some point been so caught up in our relationship, that we have lost our identity.

Maybe you have lost touch with your contacts, or you no longer have time to engage in those things you love doing, or you feel that you have done certain things that made you compromise on many occasions that you no longer feel the union represents who you claim to be.

If you find out that you've lost who you are in the relationship, begin creating time for yourself and doing what you cherish before your relationship. A successful relationship is the one where two-persons reside, can complement each other and live amicably alongside each other. It's so imperative to make out time for your relationships as well as the other important people in your life because you'll always need them in the course of time.

However, if you think you have done everything possible to make the relationship work, and these changes have not yielded the desired intentions (for example, you have abandoned all your expectations to follow your partner because you felt this was the only way to keep the relationship intact), then you need to figure out whether this relationship will really ever serve you both.

Naturally, this is not an easy conclusion to arrive at, but the aloneness you feel from not being who you are because you live with the wrong person, will always not be as good as the type of loneliness you feel because you're single.

This of course is not only because you can at least discover your identity again and live your life the way you want it, but because there's still hope that you will find that right person who will complement you and provide you with love and protection as a result of being the person you are.

iii.    Make the first move

Never lose your battle before the fight begins. Do not suffer depression without making a move to share your feelings with your partner. Share your thoughts with him about your loneliness. This may inspire him to share his version of problems, his tensions or disappointments in life. Perhaps he/she, too, is going through loneliness related issues or is having a rough time with his relationships that he shares with you without you noticing.

Yes, it can be difficult to make the first move, but your ego won't let you do that, but when you think about it, you will discover that it is actually worth the effort since you want to stop being lonely. So, take the bold step, approach your partner, and come together, otherwise, the distance will get farther. It isn't going to help matters if you are going to be in a gulf. Even if your partner is to take the blame, make the first attempt. Start easing out by engaging her in simple things like "how was your day like at work" or perhaps talk about any current local news or simply offer her a late-night ice cream. Give her a hug or a peck when you leave for office the following day. If you think that you are at fault and she has been keeping you at a distance, then be humble and apologize.

iv.    Express your emotions

It is extremely difficult to pretend that relationship problems are going to be over until and unless the partners timely express their emotions towards each other and speak to each other in a proper way. Hence, ensure that the conversation is frank and both of you speak honestly. If you have been feeling lonely, say so in an open atmosphere and say why you feel that way. There are chances that your partner will listen and respond positively, and you two can resolve the whole issue. If you are not the speaking type, then write to him about your feelings. You can email or use texts but choose the right words that are not offensive or provoke a fight. Use the words that will prove the sincerity of heart.

You may be disappointed that your partner isn't fulfilling your every need and though there are things we all expect from our partners (for example, faithfulness, love, and frankness) there are certain things we shouldn't expect our partners to do for us.

Even though your relationship should contribute to certain fulfillment, your partner cannot be hundred percent responsible for your happiness. Of course, they should make us feel happy, but we need to be happy inside ourselves first. And the same goes for our self-image, having their love shouldn't be the determinant factor whether we find ourselves loveable or not.

Putting this expectation upon our partner will not only place impractical expectations on them but eventually, it will cause you to feel disappointed when they're unable to fulfill that emptiness inside of you; resulting in you being lonely in the relationship.

If you suffer from low self-esteem, there are many things you can do about it, which will not only help you have a happier life but will make you strengthen your relationship and put you on equal footing.

If you don't already, dedicate time to yourself every day to meditate and be conscious of the negative thoughts and feelings that are weighing down your sense of worth.

v. Make plans

Loneliness issue mostly manifests when couples don't spend enough quality time together. Although it is appreciated that the present-day routines are quite hectic and tedious, but that shouldn't be the reason to ignore your relationships. You may plan for a short weekend trip to go for a date but make sure you spend a good time together. This will help you both create more recollections and will open up the opportunity for further communication as you will have enough commonness and topics to talk about.

## vi.    Be productive

Never let your professional life get affected by your personal life. Get busy with your professional life and certainly, you will slowly forget about your loneliness. Make contacts and interact with friends, keep yourself busy with work of any kind so far it keeps you away from thinking about loneliness. Be ready to organize something that will bring people of like-minds together mainly for interactive reasons rather than for economic reasons. Join career minded society where you will meet colleagues in the same profession. A career will be of great help to keep you busy so that you focus on priorities in life

An idle mind, they say, is the devil's workshop. Loneliness in a relationship can also occur if you aren't engaged in something that will fetch you money. In all sincerity, your partner cannot offer you all his time, and it will not be fair to expect much from him. Take up some work or explore your areas of interest and get yourself busy. Full-Time or part-time work will get you engaged, and when you are fully engaged, it is not likely you will be thinking about loneliness. At the end of the days/weeks job, you will be tired to the extent that you will be looking for a resting place. With this, you will overcome loneliness and become happy again. It is important to be creative and productive to make peace with the soundless ghost.

# CHAPTER FIVE: Other Tips to Deal with Loneliness in A Relationship

I.    Try to engage him/her on interesting conversations and stop engaging him/her on transactional conversations. Be inspired to approach your spouse him/her opinion about the football match played the previous evening.   Listen attentively to your spouse's response and ask a follow-up question. It is natural that your spouse may be reluctant to respond, but eventually, your patience will pay-off.

II.    Change your orientation.   Find out what your partner likes and dislikes. Try to see her activity from her own perspective and suspend your judgmental attitude for the meantime.   Perhaps by seeing your partner's activity through her eyes, unnecessary arguments may not be started, and you can actually enjoy the things she likes in her own way.

III. You both should experience something new. It may be a good idea to spend some time with friends outside your home. Perhaps, watching a movie, football match, physical exercise or go for a swim. When you come back to the house, you will have a lot to talk about and tell each other. Since you both are partakers, serious arguments are unlikely to arise when you narrate your experiences from each other's point of view.

In a similar way, each partner can take some time off, visiting other friends, and accepting external invitations for birthday parties or other unrelated events. It may not only be time to recharge but to see things without your partner in the picture.

IV. Do carry out some tasks together. For some couples that do not spend time together, invite your partner to the kitchen to cook together or to the launderette to see your clothes washed, or to the shopping mall. Doing something together may, perhaps spice up the relationship a little bit. For some couples, it is of fun to shop together and see the results of the things they did together. The question of nagging shouldn't arise since both of them made the decision to pick the things they bought from the supermarket.

V.      Pay attention to your spouse.

By giving your partner undivided attention and not pre-judging him/her actions, you create a safe environment to talk freely and open up to areas of your that were hitherto considered a no-go area. When a partner is too judgmental or is nagging a lot, it is always difficult to express one's feelings. It is very annoying to begin to criticize your partner even before you have the chance to hear him/her out.

VI.    Act foolishly sometimes.

Don't be too hard on your spouse at all times.  Soften a bit and pretend to be a fool. You may notice in life that friendship is sweet when one partner is soft while the other may be hard, exercising superiority or masculinity.   If you find out that your partner is too pushy, or hard to please, by all means, calm down and pretend that all is well so that peace reigns.  If you understand your partner well, use this approach to bring things under control before things get out of hand.   Speak to your partner afterward in the conducive atmosphere when it is expected he or she would listen.

# CHAPTER SIX: Building Intimacy with Your Partner

Building and maintaining intimacy in a relationship takes time, and it takes some folks longer than others. Often, the more effort you put in at developing intimacy in your relationship, the more rewarding it is. But first things first, let us examine ourselves and see where we stand and then, how to approach not to be lonely but remain connected to our partners.

It is also important at this stage to dig dipper into what relationships mean so that we know which intimate relationship we are addressing.

## The Perfect Relationship

A perfect relationship can't mean the same thing to everybody because the word is loosely used in most cases.

What kind of relationship do you have? Friendship is fundamentally why couple falls in love. Some couples want to live together and still maintain their independence; others want to spend a lot of time in each other's company, while others prefer to be bound by law.

Everyone manages relationships in their way. It's important to make some distinctions between different types of relationships.

## Devoted relationships

This means being committed to the relationship and deciding together on the rules of the game and accepting them. It normally translates into being loyal and 'exclusive' to each other. You don't make out or have sex with anyone except your partner.

## Open relationships

The open relationship allows each other to date as many people as possible and/or have sex with them as he/she chooses. It means they maintain honesty with their partners about sleeping with other people and naturally don't notice the bad side of it and it doesn't affect the relationship.

## Live-in relationships

In some cultures, it's acceptable for couples to live together without being married.

Partners may choose to live together without getting married for reasons known to them, which in some cases could be because they want to maintain their single status, or because they're the same-sex and can't marry legally in most of the countries in Africa.

## Married relationships

Marriage is a union between a man and a woman within the framework of the law. The decision to marry is a decision made solely by the two people, some time together with some family members.

In this context, I am going to exclude the "open relationships" since, in this kind of relationship, intimacy in the real sense can't be observed in each of the partners they keep. But before I talk about how couples can build intimacy in their relationship to avert the incidence of loneliness, I would advise some couples to free themselves from the shackles of loneliness.

## Release yourself of a feeling of loneliness:

First and foremost, try to get out of where you are stuck in loneliness. In the research of father and daughter, psychologists Drs. Robert and Lisa Firestone, they discovered that some people have some negative thoughts toward themselves that they are "different from other people. This self-restricting attitude can keep you stuck in a cycle of loneliness for a long time. Your negative inner voices often try to overshadow you from challenging yourself to step outside your comfort zone. When you become aware of these self-attacks, you mustn't allow them to manipulate how you live your life. Acknowledge your feelings of loneliness and isolation by saying to yourself "I feel lonely right now, but I am not going to give in to my critical inner voice and beat myself up about it." Instead, you should take more positive actions and liberate yourself from the circle of isolation and loneliness

Here are suggestions on how to build intimacy with your partner to combat the feelings of loneliness while in a relationship.

## Celebrate the great occasions in your relationship.

Tell your partner, in words and some other ways, how much you love and care about them. Open up to your partner what you value about them and regarding the relationship. Let them know it both in words and actions, never assume they are already aware. Everyone likes to be told that they are appreciated and cared about.

Talk openly about your feelings and what you would like to see in the relationship.

If you discover overtime after your relationship started that you are feeling lonely sometimes, it is time to speak openly about your observation. It may be that you are fully engaged during the day, and naturally, when your partner returns home very tired, she/he doesn't give you the chance to have a few minutes conversation before retiring for the night. Even though you appreciate your partner and respect him/her, you can't continue in a relationship you are more or less abandoned in the cold. That is the reason you must speak up to let him/her understand what you pass through daily.

## Create opportunities for intimacy.

Take a trip to be alone to concentrate on one another and your relationship. Attempt to arrange a daily evening, day or weekend for the 2 of you to be alone.

Accept that your relationship can have ups and downs but don't relent. Make the extra effort in exploring new ways of finding a deeper level of intimacy. These moments don't need to be grand gestures of affection. Taking time, even little moments, over a cup of coffee can add a spice in your relationship.

**Go to bed together.**

People work out what is good for themselves. If you and your partner seem to have opposite schedules or have different routines before you go to bed, try to work it out so that your schedule can coincide with your partner. If possible, create a routine together and let your end-of-day winding down become a space for you to reconnect.

**Intimacy in a relationship**

Some relationships just lose their spark because one of the partners is becoming overtly inquisitive. When you are the less busy one, you begin imagining things because your partner often comes up with the excuse of late hour meetings. Consequently, instead of showing empathy, you start avoiding your partner and thereby begin to feel a loss of connection and affection which you once cherished. You may see yourself going through the emotional anguish and isolation. The solution to stop being lonely is to pretend nothing has happened and go back to your partner, rekindling those things that keep you connected. Go back to your spouse, show empathy, show deeply how you love him, make his meals on time and don't go to bed until he comes home. Show concern about his whereabout, particularly those nights he is late from work.

Let your partner or spouse know your feelings: It's important to let them know how you feel. You and your partner may be able to work out things together for the good of the relationship. For example, both of you may decide it's time to plan a weekend getaway or a package holiday. Even a walk in the seaside together could help relieve a sense of loneliness. Making out even a small chunk of time to focus attention on each other may bring relief and a sense of belonging ultimately.

**Spend some time with friends**

"Simply because you are lonely in your relationship, doesn't mean you feel the same when you're among friends or loved ones." If the company of others will help you in your lonely relationship, then make efforts to do more things with others. It may be about helping out your friends or keeping them company. See if these moments of connectedness can help ease your feelings of loneliness with your partner or spouse.

## Get occupied outside your relationship

Spending less time around your spouse or partner can help reduce the feeling of loneliness and may help the relationship. Volunteer opportunities, hobby clubs, professional associations, and jogging, biking, swimming, fitness exercise and workout groups, are all possible ways to keep you focused elsewhere and keep you happy, outside the scope of your relationship.

## Unhealthy communication patterns

Lack of mutual communication is a common reason for feeling lonely in relationships. Reflect on your own whether you have already some unhealthy communication patterns, these patterns may make one or both of you fail to listen with respect, share openly, and respond with interest to each other. For example, as you feel ignored, or feel like your spouse doesn't care about or understand what you are communicating, there is a tendency that you will stop talking to each other; gradually, walls start to rise, and you will get used to living emotionally separate lives.

## Sign of inferiority complex

No matter how good your spouse is intellectually, never you feel inferior to the level of showing signs of inferiority. If you are married, it is the more reason why both of you is one and equal—even though the man is the head of the family. Yes, his or her friends may be professors or senators but you shouldn't feel dumb when having conversation with those people. Don't be isolated, feel rejected or intimidated by the presence of your spouse high-class friends, join in any conversation when those of your spouse friends come around. If you shy away from your spouse's friends because of any reason, your spouse will always be uncomfortable taking you out for big occasions. Once your spouse is not free asking you out for big events, your marriage may be on the line.

The reason you should join them in any conversation and get your point of view across is that you may feel the same way if you join another group elsewhere. For example, if you are co-opted to a committee in your organization answerable to the board of directors and you are to speak for your committee in a board meeting, would you shy away from your duty?

## Engage in something meaningful

If you are feeling lonely and you are jobless, depending fully on your spouse for financial support, you aren't being fair to yourself. Make a serious effort to get occupied with something. Your spouse will appreciate you more if you are busy. Idle mind they say is the devil's workshop. Intimacy within marriage can't be developed if one partner lazy about. It could well be that the jobless partner is feeling lonely because he/she can't have his/her partner until late in the night every day. So, for you to build the intimacy that has the chance to last, both the partners must be fully engaged.

Experiment new skills, sign up for a cooking class, online course or volunteer at a community project in your area.

## Make new friends

Get to know more people outside your home and get along with them. There are great people in churches, recreation clubs, professional associations and volunteer organizations. Join a group with similar interests to you. It is better to be in a group doing something you enjoy doing together than to exclude yourself and be having the inner self-pity about your predicament.

You can be noticed in a group if you engage in a project and accomplish it excellently. In this case, it is not you that will look for people; great personalities will be looking for you.

## Speak out

Don't allow yourself to die in silence. If you're not sure what to do when you are lonely, speak to someone you can trust. Sometimes it is more appropriate to reach out to other people who might be in a better position to help you in your loneliness. It could be your partner, but if you don't feel he/she is the one, approach a close friend or family member, otherwise meet a professional.

# CHAPTER SEVEN: Making a Room for Intimacy

Always express your love for your partner in words and action. For example, welcome your partner from work with a kiss or a hug and find out how his/her day was.

Show gratitude for small things - For example, helping your partner in small things, say thank you darling and a hug or peg.

Find random moments to reach out and connect. Tell him love stories you read in your primary school books immediately after dinner.

Be an active listener. As you listen, make eye contact and ask appropriate questions to show that you are attentive.

Be open to your partner – tell her about your day and how you handled your office tasks. Talk about your challenges and breakthroughs.

Do some big/new things together – Celebrate his birthday in a big way beyond his expectations. Or book for a package holiday when he/she is only expecting a day trip to the seaside.

Make it difficult for your partner to work out from the relationship. Learn about your partner, understand him/her inside out and treat him/her in a way they would love to be treated.

Create an opportunity for physical intimacy. For example, play and dance for him his best song, invite him to join the dance and afterwards lead him away for a steam bath.

Support your spouse at the slightest opportunity. In times of sadness, give her/him your full support both in cash and in-kind.

Don't always depend on your partner for financial support even though he/she may be willing always to lend a helping hand.

Surprise him/her sometimes. Buy expensive gifts or defend and stand by him/her in the moments of trials.

Share your daily routines such as washing or cooking.

Communicate regularly even when you are in the office, it is sufficient to send an SMS to say, "Thank you again for taking good care of the kids, I will be back home in an hour".

# CHAPTER EIGHT: Notable Facts About Intimacy and Loneliness

Intimacy in a relationship is a feeling of being close and showing an emotional connection. It means having the ability to share a wide range of thoughts, feelings, and experiences with your partner. It involves living the life of openness, honesty, oneness, and let you know your thoughts and emotions, hopes and desires and what your dreams are.

Intimacy is developed over time and calls for both parties in the relationship to put in some efforts to make it work. Being intimate with someone you've fallen in love with is one of the good aspects of a relationship. In addition to emotional and sexual intimacy, you'll be able to have intimacy intellectually, recreationally, financially, spiritually, creatively (for example, doing interior decoration for your home) and sometimes marital upheavals (working as a team throughout hard times).

## Intimacy in relationships

Intimacy is achieved when we tend to be close to our partner, tolerate one another and be reassured that we are loved and accepted for who we are. For many couples, 'making love' involves a way of intimacy and emotional closeness. An intimate relationship is beyond sex and involves trust and being vulnerable with one another.

But it's vital to share a full array of emotions with a partner; otherwise, some folks may begin to feel lonely and isolated notwithstanding how good their lovemaking experiences may be. Explore other ways in which to share the love and warm-heartedness without sex. Often, the more other ways you are intimate with one another beside sex, the more fulfilling their sex life becomes.

## Difficulties in developing intimacy

Some couples realize that it is an uphill task attaining full intimacy in their relationship, others will find that even after working hard to achieve intimacy, it appears to slip away. Several factors stand in the way of achieving intimacy in a relationship, this is often the results of common issues such as:

• **Communication breakdown** – if the couple is not communicating the way they should to each other about their feelings and needs are and if you feel being misunderstood most of the time your partner speaks of her needs, then how can an intimate relationship be established? If you don't feel listened to by your partner then intimacy will be difficult to actualize and maintain. It's vital to speak to your partner about what her needs are and how she feels about the current issues concerning family matters. Giving your partner a listening ear alone will create a sense of connection and intimation.

• **Conflict** – if there's an existing conflict in your relationship, it will be more difficult to develop intimacy outright without first and foremost settling the ongoing conflict amicably. It's not an easy thing to feel free with someone who nags you now and then on the slightest provocation. Anger, hurt, bitterness, lack of trust, or the disposition of being unappreciated will all affect intimacy.

• **Practical day to day problems** – practical issues and life stressors like outstanding and mounting bills, pressures at work, concern regarding kids, or simply being too busy to connect will affect intimacy. There are times in a relationship when the individual needs have to be sacrificed for the needs of the couple. One of those times is when the closeness of the relationship is at stake. So it is important to carve out time together even if it is just for a few minutes over a cup of tea. Few minutes of being together are likely to add up to a greater feeling of intimacy.

• **Abuse or violence** – intimacy is greatly threatened once one partner uses superior power in an inappropriate way over the other. Abuse of power or the use of violence in a relationship damages trust and signals that the relationship is going to hit the rocks, sooner or later

All relationships have one form of barrier or the other to intimacy. it's only natural for couples to figure along to beat these barriers.

# Conclusion

Some of us go through loneliness in relationships. Whatever are the causes, they are generally attributed to the feelings of disconnection from your partner and/or yourself. Don't ever think loneliness can go away if you do nothing to stamp it out of your life. You must try to relate your lonely feelings to the people you can trust – family and friends, and talk it through with your partner. That is the beginning of solving your loneliness problem. It is said, "a problem shared is a problem half solved." If you don't address the truth and root causes of the problem, you will end up having the feeling locked up in your emotions as though you are the only person in the world.

Intimacy can be achieved in a relationship to combat loneliness. But it is not one-sided task but a task for the couple to tackle together. It is a balancing act between the man and the woman, whether they are in a committed relationship, uncommitted relationship or just marriage of convenience.

# Other Books by the Same Author

1. <u>200 Ways to Seduce Your Husband:</u> How to Boost Your Marriage Libido and Actually Enjoy Sex: A Couple's Intimacy Guide

2. <u>232 Questions for Couples</u>: Romantic Relationship Conversation Starters for Connecting, Building Trust, and Emotional Intimacy

3. <u>Communication in Marriage:</u> How to Communicate Effectively With Your Spouse, Build Trust and Rekindle Love

4. <u>Anger Management in Marriage:</u> Ways to Control Your Emotions, Get Healed of Hurts & Respond to Offenses (Overcome Bad Temper)

5. <u>100 Ways to Cultivate Intimacy in Your Marriage</u>: How to Improve Communication, Build Trust and Rekindle Love

6. <u>40 Bible Verses to Pray Over Your Husband and Marriage:</u> Powerful Scriptural Prayers for Protection, Guidance, Wisdom, Companionship, Commitment, Healing, and Deliverance

7. <u>Sexual Intimacy in Marriage:</u> 100 Facts Nobody Ever Told You About Sex and Romance

8. <u>How to Build Trust in a Relationship:</u> Powerful Ways to Rebuild Effective Communication, Resolve Conflict, Improve Intimacy, And Avoid Betrayal

Manufactured by Amazon.ca
Bolton, ON

27806423R00046